13 PRACTICAL STEPS TO BUILD A STRONG FAMILY CULTURE.

BY

Dr TIMOTHY KESSINGTON

approval from the publisher or creator.

TABLE OF CONTENTS

ABOUT THE AUTHOR

INTRODUCTION.

TABLE OF CONTENTS

13 PRACTICAL STEPS TO BUILD A STRONG FAMILY CULTURE.

INTRODUCTION

CHAPTER 1. What is family culture?

CHAPTER 2. Why is family culture important?

CHAPTER 3. Identify what your family culture is.

CHAPTER 4. Make it a habit.

CHAPTER 5. Cultivate the value of each behaviour.

CHAPTER 6. Reiterate your family's views.

CHAPTER 7. Create family rituals and customs.

CHAPTER 8. Communicate often and freely.

CHAPTER 9. Show respect and gratitude.

CHAPTER 10. Foster a feeling of responsibility and independence.

CHAPTER 11. Prioritize quality time together.

CHAPTER 12. Adapt to change.

CHAPTER 13. Commonly asked questions about developing a solid marital culture.

CONCLUSION

ABOUT THE AUTHOR

Dr. TIMOTHY KESSINGTON is a licensed psychologist in the state of Texas. he is a certified counselor on marriage and relationship/mental health. He is passionate to the core to see people in relationships happy and couples achieve the best out of every relationship.

INTRODUCTION

I adore visiting my school's family day. It's a happy moment to see all families coming around and supporting their children, their siblings, or their nieces and nephews.

School is one of the finest venues to experience the core of family culture. Everyone, ranging from the youngsters to other members of the family, looks forward to being a part of the family day. After all, it provides the elder generation a fantastic opportunity to recall their school days.

Some families arrive in colour-coordinated outfits. Other families even act together on stage, while others are incredibly traditional. One thing is evident; they all have their own family culture.

CHAPTER 1. What is family culture?

Family culture is a collection of your family beliefs, standards, ethics, and customs that your family adheres to; some of these are handed down from generation to generation.

So, what is a family culture? It is what makes your family distinctive as a unit. It is your identity; it is what makes you recognize that you believe your family doesn't have an "identity," you are incorrect. Every household has this!

Does your family pray together before sleeping? Does your family enjoy touring? Does your family love melody? Does your family enjoy reading? Does your family like crafts and skills? Does your family have everyday or weekly family dinners?

I know of families who graduated from school at the same institution or college, and they would go out to watch their school's games versus their rival teams. I know some families that always go on vacation every summer. I know several families that are constantly joining fun runs.

These are some of the instances of family customs that are crucial in developing successful families. These family culture examples throughout the globe encourage us to establish one for ourselves, too, which may help to create a strong family.

CHAPTER 2. Why is family culture important?

Family and culture are interwoven. Yes, your family culture is vital because, like your identity, family culture is what makes your family an intrinsic part of your life.

Family disputes and obstacles highlight exactly how significant family culture is, like in the case of sibling rivalry.

Family psychologists and therapists highlight the necessity of developing and nurturing a family culture.

When siblings quarrel, it's neither the frequency nor the severity of those disputes that characterize sibling relationships. Family civilization and ceremony create tiny moments that make up for the challenges and disagreements.

By developing our own family culture, we can safeguard our bond with our family.

Family culture enables us to understand how significant the tiny things are. Through our family culture, we can come back to something when our exterior world gets too demanding and too stressful.

Family culture is what makes our house a home to come back to. establishing your own family culture is crucial for establishing strong family values, which ultimately assist us to remain connected and strong in difficult times. Here are the basic steps you may take to develop your own family culture.

CHAPTER 3. Identify what your family culture is.

Families in various cultures work differently. So, it is vital to understand what culture dominates in your household without comparing it with others. Family ideas and values must be evaluated individually for the benefit of the whole family.

It's not that difficult to establish what your family culture is. You may start by writing everything that appears to be a part of your lifestyle all down in bullets or via a colourful and exciting practice called mind mapping.

Mind mapping is a terrific technique to discover what additional things we might relate to the key thought. In figuring out what your family culture is, you may set your family smack in the middle of the map, and from there, attempt to offer "definitions" to your family.

You may add only basic phrases, values, or even actions that you are currently performing. You may build a separate mind map for values or activities that you would want your family to work on.

Get a huge sheet of paper, and some bright markers, and start mind mapping!

By the conclusion of this project, you will have built a spider-like structure and a sense of what your family's culture is.

CHAPTER 4. Make it a habit.

"We are what we repeatedly do."
— Will Durant, in his study of
Aristotle's Nicomachean Ethics.
After finding the things that your
family members link with you all
being a family, you can now
begin to maintain doing it and
making it into a habit.

CHAPTER 5. Cultivate the value of each behaviour.

So, how to develop a solid family relationship?

If one of the things that your family genuinely values is 'learning' or you intend 'learning' to be the 'traditional definition' for kids, then a Scrabble game night on Fridays may be something that you could do as a means to reinforce the meaning of this value.

We do not merely stop at developing them into habits. We

consistently reaffirm this because there is value to it.

Having a family culture is vital because it offers you and your children a loving safety net when things go rough.

The purpose of building a family culture is not to generate a list of things to do. It's about discovering what your family believes in, and what your family importance are.

As your lives continue to go ahead, you will find out that some of your ideals or some of the activities that you have built as a tradition don't match your lifestyle anymore. That's alright. There are certain activities that you will grow out of. But do not forget that the key component of these activities you've established is the inherent values that your family takes away from it.

CHAPTER 6. Reiterate your family's views.

One key step in developing a solid family culture is to identify your family's strongly-held views. Discuss with your family what beliefs are important to each member and what it means to them as a part of the home. Honesty, respect, compassion, and responsibility are some of the examples of family principles. Once you have determined these values and beliefs, be sure to model them regularly to your children.

CHAPTER 7. Create family rituals and customs.

Family rituals and customs give a feeling of continuity and connection. They might be as basic as a weekly family game night or a special holiday supper. Choose rituals and customs that are significant to your family and keep to them.

CHAPTER 8. Communicate often and freely.

Effective communication is vital for developing a solid family culture. Make sure to talk often and freely with your family members. Encourage your children to communicate their ideas and emotions with you, and be sure you actively listen to them.

CHAPTER 9. Show respect and gratitude.

Showing appreciation and thanks is a vital element of developing a good family culture. Take the time to recognize your family members' successes, large and small. Express appreciation for their contributions to the family, and be sure to say "thank you" regularly.

CHAPTER 10. Foster a feeling of responsibility and independence.

Fostering a feeling of responsibility and independence in your children is a vital element of establishing a solid family culture. Encourage your children to take on age-appropriate duties, such as housework and care for their things.

This will help kids develop a feeling of pride and ownership in their contributions to the family.

CHAPTER 11. Prioritize quality time together.

Quality time together is vital for developing a solid family culture. Make sure to emphasize family time, such as family trips, vacations, and lunches together. Make use of technology to keep connected with family members who reside far away.

CHAPTER 12. Adapt to change.

Finally, it is crucial to be adaptive and flexible in the face of change. Family dynamics vary with time, and it is necessary to be ready to adjust to meet the existing circumstances for the comfort and safety of each family member. Seeking professional assistance via marital therapy may also help couples become adaptable to shifting circumstances and dynamics within the family.

CHAPTER 13. Commonly asked questions about developing a solid marital culture.

Here are some questions and their answers on developing a strong culture for your family and keeping it constructive throughout the years.

How can you develop a culture at home?

Building a culture at home involves purposeful work and consistency. Start by recognizing the values that are essential to your family and creating rituals or traditions that reinforce those values. Encourage open conversation, active listening, and empathy.

Set limits and standards while still allowing for individual expression and innovation. Show respect and acknowledgement for each other's efforts and successes. Celebrate milestones and important moments together. Cultivate a feeling of belonging and connection by emphasizing quality time spent together.

What is an example of family culture?

An example of family culture may be a household that values education and intellectual curiosity. They may value reading and studying, have frequent talks about current events or ideas, and promote each other's intellectual aspirations.

They may also focus priority on critical thinking and problem-solving and participate in discussions or friendly contests to foster intellectual progress. This family may have a library or specific reading place in their house, attend educational events or lectures, and seek out educational trip experiences.

CONCLUSION

Building a family culture requires work, but it can have a tremendous influence on the well-being and pleasure of everyone in the home.

By actively building rituals, communicating effectively, and emphasizing shared values, families may create a strong feeling of identity, belonging, and connection that can last through difficulties and changes. Investing in a family culture is a worthy task with long-lasting advantages.

Your family culture is what makes your family your own. Be proud of it and accept it.